Victoria Plum

Victoria Goes on a Picnic

Angela Rippon

Illustrated by Robert Dyke

Purnell

SBN 361 05581 1

First published 1983 by Purnell Books, Paulton,
Bristol, BS18 5LQ, a member of the BPCC group.
Reprinted 1985.

Made and printed in Great Britain by Purnell and Sons
(Book Production) Limited, Paulton, Bristol.

Ben Has An Idea

Benjamin Elf was lying in bed thinking about all the things he was going to have to do that day, and he wasn't very pleased about any of them. He had to clean the house, darn his socks, and do his homework. But outside the sun was shining and it was obviously going to be a lovely day. Ben thought, 'It would be a pity to waste such a glorious sunny day by staying indoors—but what can I do instead?' He thought for a moment, then threw back the bedclothes and jumped out of bed—"I know," he said, "I'll take Victoria for a tremendous picnic."

He splashed his face with water, threw on his clothes, and was careful to choose a pair of socks that only had one big hole in the toe. "If I don't take my shoes off," he said, "no one will ever see that." Then he looked in the larder to see what food he could take on the picnic. There was a very old piece of bread, a square of cheese that felt rather hard, and two apples. 'Not much of a feast there,' he thought, 'but Victoria's bound to have plenty of food—she always does.' So he picked up the two apples, put them in his pocket, and flew off to Victoria's house.

When he arrived, he found Victoria in the kitchen.

She'd been up since early morning, baking scones and cakes and a huge apple pie.

Ben sniffed the air. "Delicious," he said, "they'll be perfect for our picnic."

Victoria was confused. "What picnic?" she said. "I was cooking these for tea on Sunday."

But Ben wasn't really listening. "Don't worry about that," he said, "you've got plenty of time to make some more tomorrow. It's such a lovely day I've come to take you for a picnic. I've brought two apples, and with those scones, that cake, and that lovely apple pie, there'll be more than enough food." And with that he started to pack everything into a large basket.

Victoria could see that it was no use trying to argue with him. And after all, it was such a lovely day that it really would be nice to spend a lazy day enjoying the sunshine. So she put a clean white cloth over the food, made sure they had plates and cups, and knives and forks, and followed Ben out into the sunshine.

They made their way through the trees to the river bank. Victoria loved this part of the Great Wood. It was so peaceful here, and so pretty with the trees and the flowers, and the gentle gurgling of the clear water.

"This is just perfect," she said, and they both sat down on a grassy bank under the shade of a huge old tree. While Victoria spread the cloth and laid out their

food, Ben played a tune on his flute. Although Ben loved to play music, he wasn't really very good. But Victoria wouldn't be unkind to Ben and ask him to stop. Instead she sang quietly to herself, and Ben went on playing his flute—happy to think that his friend liked his music. The strange, squeaky notes filled the air, and it wasn't long before all the other creatures in the Great Wood heard the sound. They wondered what on earth could be making such a racket, and one by one they followed the sound through the trees to find out where such an awful noise was coming from.

The Picnic

The swift fox was the first to arrive. He ran straight to Victoria and said, "Are you all right, Victoria? It sounds as though someone is in pain."

But Victoria smiled and said in a whisper, "It's all right, it's only Ben. He's playing his flute while I get the picnic ready. Would you like to join us?"

"Oh that's all right then," said the fox, and he curled up in a patch of sunshine while Victoria finished laying out the food.

Then one by one the rest of the creatures arrived to see what was making such a strange noise. The rabbits sat shyly on the edge of the wood. The squirrels peered down from the tree tops. The mice scampered busily along the water's edge, and the butterflies floated overhead in a cloud of brilliant jewel colours of red and yellow, blue and orange. The birds all gathered in the tree tops and sang as sweetly as they could, in competition with Ben's terrible tunes. Ben of course was delighted, because he thought he had an audience who'd come to enjoy his music, so he played with even greater enthusiasm.

At last, Victoria said, "Would you all like to join our picnic?" and the animals agreed at once. Everyone knew that Victoria Plum was a wonderful cook, and they couldn't wait to sample her cakes and scones and that delicious-looking apple pie.

In no time at all everyone was eating and swopping gossip. In fact everyone was having such a lovely time, that no one noticed the huge, black rain cloud that was lurking behind the trees. Suddenly it covered the sun, and a fat heavy raindrop plopped onto the tablecloth. Then another, and another, and in seconds the sky was filled with angry rain, and all the creatures were rushing for the shelter of the trees.

Victoria looked at the picnic and cried, "All my lovely food will be ruined!"

"Don't worry," said the rabbit, "we'll save it," and all the animals rushed back to the picnic and carried the food to the safety of the trees. The birds picked up the cloth in their beaks and the fox trotted off with the basket, while Ben and Victoria sheltered under the broad leaves of a foxglove, which were so huge they were just like giant umbrellas.

Everyone stayed snug and dry while the rain pelted down, and although Victoria was glad the food was saved, she wished she had learnt enough magic to make the rain go away. But Victoria was still a very junior fairy and she could only do magic on very small things, so she waited patiently with her friends, and hoped that it wouldn't go on raining all day.

But they didn't have to wait long. Just as suddenly as the rain had started, it stopped, and everyone came out of their hiding places, to enjoy the sunshine again. Ben helped Victoria to shake the flowers dry, and together they mended the ones that had been broken by the rain.

They tied their stems with gossamer, and cast a magic spell so that the flowers could grow tall and turn their lovely faces to the sun.

After the rain had gone, everything in the wood smelt fresh and clean. The birds sang a joyous song that filled

the air, and all the creatures began dancing over the freshly washed grass. Even on the river the insects were dancing on the water.

"Come on, Victoria!" called one of the smallest mice, "why not come and join us?"

Now Victoria loved to dance, so she couldn't resist their invitation. Ben picked up his flute and joined the birds in their song, and it wasn't long before the whole of the Great Wood was echoing to the sound of music and the happy noise of creatures dancing and enjoying themselves.

Victoria was especially happy. She was so light and dainty that she floated over the grassy bank, and as she twirled round and round the tiny bells on her shoes tinkled in time with the music.

At last Victoria couldn't dance any more, she was exhausted. So she sat on the bank to catch her breath and watch the rest of the woodland creatures dancing and having fun.

Suddenly, Victoria realised that she wasn't alone. Just a few feet away in the shadow of a large stone, she could see a big, brown toad, silently watching the dancers. He had such a sad expression on his face, and as Victoria moved towards him she saw a large shiny tear form in the corner of his eye, then roll slowly over his crumpled cheek and plop onto the grass beside him.

"Please don't be so sad, Toad," said Victoria. "Come and join us. Dancing will soon make you happy."

But Toad didn't move. Instead, another tear began to

well up in his sad eyes. He wiped it away quickly, because he didn't want Victoria to see him cry. "I'd love to join you," he said. And then, looking very shy and embarrassed, he added, "But I can't dance. My friends all tell me I have two left feet. That's why I'm so sad."

Victoria looked at him kindly and had to admit that with his short arms, and his fat round body, and long, long legs, he wasn't really built for dancing. But she smiled confidently at him and said, "It's such a lot of fun—I'm sure you could dance if you tried."

Toad took Victoria's hand, and at once felt much braver. "Do you really think so?" he asked eagerly.

Victoria nodded, and together they walked towards the dance floor.

Victoria's Magic Dance

As soon as the rest of the creatures saw Victoria's dancing partner they all began to giggle and snigger behind their hands. "Oh deary me!" they whispered. "Toad thinks he's going to dance. This should be good for a laugh."

Victoria could hear them, and thought they were being very unkind. But as Toad waddled along beside her she knew in her heart that it was hopeless. He was so clumsy with his feet, it was obvious he'd never be able to dance. Victoria could see that everyone was waiting for Toad to make a fool of himself, so she was quite determined that he was going to be the best dancer the woodland creatures had ever seen. As the birds got ready to sing, Victoria slipped her hand into her apron pocket, and quickly sprinkled an extra strong mixture of fairy dust over Toad and hurriedly whispered a spell saying, "Toad, your feet are light as air. You *can* dance without a care."

The birds started the music and all the younger creatures giggled, expecting Toad to fall flat on his face. But the magic was already working. Toad took Victoria's arm, and together they began to whirl and

twirl over the ground. No one had ever seen such lovely dancing. Toad was so graceful, so light on his feet that all the animals were amazed.

"He has such grace!" said the rabbits. "As light as air!" said the butterflies. "So handsome!" said the squirrels. "I would never have believed it!" said the fox.

But Toad heard nothing except the music. He was dancing and he'd never been so happy in his life. When the music stopped Toad bowed to Victoria, and everyone started to clap.

"You were wonderful!" they all said, and suddenly everyone was crowding around Toad saying, "Please will you dance with me." But Toad was too shy to be the centre of attention for long. So he danced with the eldest lady rabbit, and the youngest lady mouse—just to be polite—then he smiled at them all, and shyly went back to the shade of his rock by the river.

At the end of the day when everyone had danced their last dance and eaten all the picnic, they went home. Victoria was the last to leave. But before she went she looked for Toad to say goodnight. He gave her a big kiss and said, "Thank you, Victoria, for making this the most wonderful day of my life. I don't know how you got me to dance—but it was magic!" and he gave her an enormous wink.

Victoria just smiled, and thought to herself how lucky it was she'd remembered to take an extra supply of fairy dust to the picnic.

In the Great Wood no one ever forgot that day. And

for years and years, whenever they gathered in their homes on dark winter evenings, the older creatures always told the story of how they'd seen the best dancer in the world on the day when Toad danced with the fairy, Victoria Plum.